EXPLORING THE STATES

Colorado

THE CENTENNIAL STATE

by Emily Schnobrich

BELLWETHER MEDIA • MINNEAPOLIS, MN

Note to Librarians, Teachers, and Parents:

Blastoff! Readers are carefully developed by literacy experts and combine standards-based content with developmentally appropriate text.

Level 1 provides the most support through repetition of high-frequency words, light text, predictable sentence patterns, and strong visual support.

Level 2 offers early readers a bit more challenge through varied simple sentences, increased text load, and less repetition of high-frequency words.

Level 3 advances early-fluent readers toward fluency through increased text and concept load, less reliance on visuals, longer sentences, and more literary language.

Level 4 builds reading stamina by providing more text per page, increased use of punctuation, greater variation in sentence patterns, and increasingly challenging vocabulary.

Level 5 encourages children to move from "learning to read" to "reading to learn" by providing even more text, varied writing styles, and less familiar topics.

Whichever book is right for your reader, Blastoff! Readers are the perfect books to build confidence and encourage a love of reading that will last a lifetime!

This edition first published in 2014 by Bellwether Media, Inc.

No part of this publication may be reproduced in whole or in part without written permission of the publisher. For information regarding permission, write to Bellwether Media, Inc., Attention: Permissions Department, 5357 Penn Avenue South, Minneapolis, MN 55419.

Library of Congress Cataloging-in-Publication Data

Schnobrich, Emily.
 Colorado / by Emily Schnobrich.
     pages cm. – (Blastoff! readers. Exploring the states)
 Includes bibliographical references and index.
 Summary: "Developed by literacy experts for students in grades three through seven, this book introduces young readers to the geography and culture of Colorado"–Provided by publisher.
 ISBN 978-1-62617-005-6 (hardcover : alk. paper)
 1. Colorado–Juvenile literature. I. Title.
 F776.3.S33 2013
 978.8–dc23
                                                                                       2013013574

Table of Contents

Where Is Colorado?

Colorado is located in the western United States. Wyoming is its neighbor to the north. Nebraska hugs its northeastern corner. To the east lies Kansas. Oklahoma and New Mexico border Colorado to the south. In the southwest, Colorado touches the corner of Arizona. Utah is its western neighbor.

The towering Rocky Mountains cover half of Colorado. The other half is part of the **Great Plains**. Denver, the capital city, lies between the two regions in north-central Colorado.

Utah

Arizona

Wyoming

Nebraska

● Fort Collins

Denver
★ ● Aurora

Colorado

● Colorado Springs

Kansas ⟶

Oklahoma

New Mexico

History

Native Americans such as the Puebloans, Arapaho, and Cheyenne were the first Colorado residents. In 1803, the United States bought much of Colorado in the **Louisiana Purchase**. Explorers began to map the land. People came in the late 1800s to search for gold and silver. They left lonely **ghost towns** behind. In the 1900s, Colorado became the home of the Air Force Academy and other government programs.

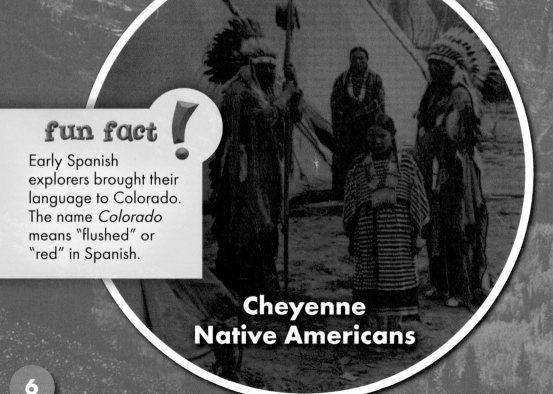

fun fact !

Early Spanish explorers brought their language to Colorado. The name *Colorado* means "flushed" or "red" in Spanish.

Cheyenne Native Americans

Colorado Timeline!

1706:   Juan de Ulibarri claims the Colorado region for Spain.

1803:   The United States buys eastern Colorado in the Louisiana Purchase.

1833:   American explorers set up Bent's Fort as part of the fur trade.

1848:   The United States gains control of western Colorado after the Mexican-American War.

1858:   Settlers discover gold in the South Platte River.

1876:   Colorado becomes the thirty-eighth state.

1879:   Large deposits of silver are discovered in Leadville and Aspen. This marks the beginning of the Silver Boom.

1958:   The U.S. Air Force Academy opens near Colorado Springs.

1999:   A deadly shooting at Columbine High School shocks the nation.

Bent's Fort

Mexican-American War

U.S. Air Force Academy

The Land

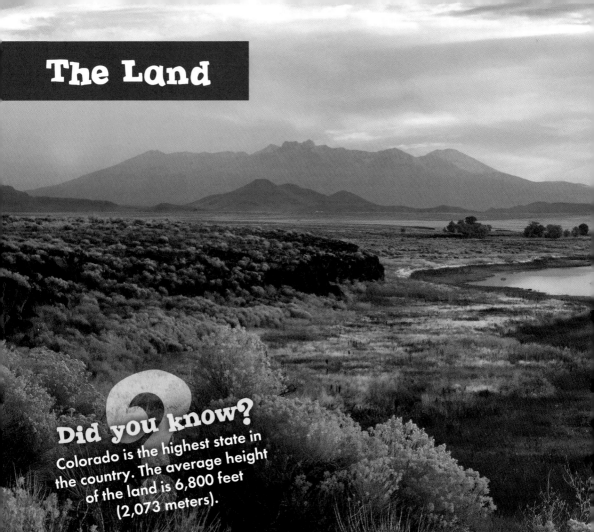

Did you know?
Colorado is the highest state in the country. The average height of the land is 6,800 feet (2,073 meters).

The Colorado landscape varies greatly across the state. The southern Rocky Mountains rise in western Colorado. Tall hills, deep valleys, and **plateaus** run along the border with Utah. The eastern half of Colorado is mostly flat. Dry, grassy **plains** cover stretches of sandstone, limestone, and other rock.

Rio Grande

Colorado's Climate
average °F

spring
Low: 33°
High: 62°

summer
Low: 54°
High: 85°

fall
Low: 33°
High: 64°

winter
Low: 14°
High: 42°

A lush, hilly area called the Colorado Piedmont separates the mountainous west from the eastern plains. It is home to many of Colorado's large cities. The Arkansas, South Platte, Colorado, and Rio Grande are Colorado's main rivers. Many smaller waterways and lakes also cover the state.

Rocky Mountains

The majestic Rocky Mountains extend south from Canada and almost touch Mexico. In Colorado, the Rockies run through the western part of the state. Their jagged peaks are some of Colorado's most beautiful features. Snowy Mount Elbert is the state's highest point at 14,433 feet (4,399 meters).

At Rocky Mountain National Park, people hike among the tall peaks. Many climb to the top of Longs Peak. Its **summit** is the size of a football field! Cool lakes, deep green valleys, and sunny meadows lie below. In the summer, people camp beneath the bright stars. In winter, visitors snowshoe and ski in the powdery mountain snow.

Mount Elbert

fun fact

Butterflies of all kinds fly through the park. The white Rocky Mountain Parnassian can survive in the cold, windy heights of the mountains.

prairie dogs

The eastern plains and Colorado Piedmont are animal playgrounds. Prairie dogs, jackrabbits, and rattlesnakes make their homes in the short grasses there. Coyotes, deer, and bison roam the hills nearby. In the mountainous west, bighorn sheep navigate steep cliffs. Pikas and marmots scurry over rocks.

Did you know?
Prairie dogs live in large groups called "towns." They communicate in a complex language of squeaks and barks.

jackrabbit

pika

bison

Cottonwood trees, cactuses, and prickly poppies grow well in the plains' dry climate. In the **foothills** bloom mariposa lilies, fiery Indian paintbrushes, and larkspurs. Oak and mahogany trees are also found there. Up in the mountains, pine, fir, and spruce trees cover the peaks. Dwarf shrubs and alpine forget-me-nots thrive in the highest areas.

Landmarks

Colorado boasts beautiful national forests and state parks for exploring. In winter, skiers and snowboarders crowd the snowy cities of Vail and Aspen. The Durango-Silverton steam engine carries passengers to charming old mining towns. These little communities are full of shops, mountain views, and history.

Near Colorado Springs, young men and women learn to fly military planes at the United States Air Force Academy. Visitors can admire the Cadet Chapel, see military **memorials**, and glimpse life at the Academy. Natural **hot springs** are scattered throughout Colorado. People relax in the toasty water while surrounded by fluffy snow.

Durango-Silverton steam engine

fun fact

The southwestern tip of Colorado touches the corners of Arizona, Utah, and New Mexico. At Four Corners, visitors can stand in all four states at once!

United States Air Force Academy
Cadet Chapel

Denver

Colorado's capital, Denver, is just east of the Rocky Mountains. The city was settled by people seeking gold in the 1850s. Today, Denver is known as the Mile High City. At 5,280 feet (1,609 meters) above sea level, it is exactly one mile high.

Did you know?
Denver had a rough beginning. During the first years of its existence, a fire and a flood destroyed the city!

Denver Botanic Gardens

Denver is a goldmine for outdoor activities. Nature lovers can roam its blooming Botanic Gardens or visit the elephants at the Denver Zoo. Parks, bicycle paths, and hiking trails cross the rocky city. Visitors can learn about Denver's wild past at the grave of Buffalo Bill. This Wild West showman was famous all over the world.

Working

Colorado is one of the top cattle producers in the nation. Farmers also raise pigs and sheep. Corn, wheat, and hay are Colorado's main crops. Miners dig for oil, natural gas, and coal across the state.

Some Coloradans build weapons and spacecraft for the United States government. Factory workers make sugar from the state's sugar beets. Others build machinery and electronics. Most Coloradans have **service jobs**. Each year, they serve millions of **tourists** at restaurants, ski resorts, and outdoor attractions.

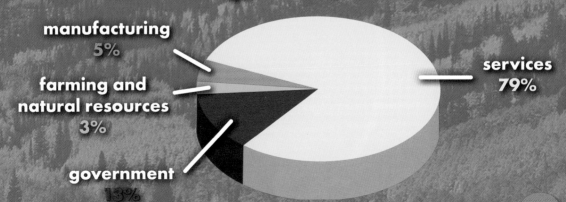

Where People Work in Colorado

- manufacturing 5%
- farming and natural resources 3%
- government 13%
- services 79%

Playing

Colorado's varied landscape welcomes all kinds of outdoor adventures. Skiing and snowboarding are some of the most popular pastimes. Coloradans also hike, snowshoe, and rock climb in the mountains. When the snow melts, they ride the river rapids on large rafts or go fishing on the banks.

Music lovers enjoy outdoor concerts at the natural **amphitheater** in Red Rocks Park. Coloradans also go to operas and ballets at the Denver Performing Arts Complex. Sports fans root for the state's professional hockey, baseball, basketball, and football teams.

Red Rocks amphitheater

Skiing is a big part of Colorado's history. Early settlers sometimes delivered the mail by skiing from house to house.

Denver Omelet

Ingredients:

- 3 large eggs
- 2 tablespoons butter
- 1/4 cup chopped onion
- 1/4 cup green bell peppers, chopped
- 1/4 cup cooked ham, cubed
- 1/4 cup shredded cheddar cheese
- 1/2 teaspoon salt
- 1/2 teaspoon pepper

Directions:

1. Melt butter in a large nonstick skillet. Sauté onions, peppers, and ham in the butter until veggies are tender but crisp. Remove from skillet.

2. In a small bowl, whip eggs. Add salt and pepper.

3. Slowly pour the eggs into the skillet. Let sit, then start to gently push cooked egg to the center. Let uncooked egg move to the outside but leave no gaps.

4. When eggs are mostly cooked, add onions, peppers, ham, and cheese onto half of the omelet. Fold omelet over filling. Cook until cheese is melted, flipping once.

Denver Omelet

Did you know?
Colorado is known for the Denver Omelet, a dish of cooked eggs with ham, onions, and green peppers. Some believe this was a quick and filling meal for cowboys on the Western trail.

Green Chili

Mexican food is a big deal in southern Colorado. Hungry Coloradans often pick up burritos or tacos for lunch. They also love a Mexican-style stew called Green Chili. This thick soup is filled with pork, tomatoes, and peppers.

Many cooks in Colorado like to use ingredients that are grown in their own communities. In fall and winter, Coloradans roast squash and pumpkins. They pick berries, cherries, and sweet corn to eat in the summer. Peaches and apples are baked into pies and other desserts in the fall.

Festivals

Coloradans are proud of their winters. In Breckenridge, snow lovers from around the world compete in the International Snow Sculpture Championship. Teams have five days to build a creative snow sculpture that will dazzle judges. At the Steamboat Springs Winter Carnival, there are ski jumping competitions, fireworks, and parades.

Farmers show off their best sheep, cows, and horses at the National Western Stock Show in Denver. Cowboys and cowgirls impress crowds at the Stock Show **Rodeo**. Some of them even ride horses **bareback**!

National Western
Stock Show
parade

International Snow
Sculpture Championship

Ancestral Puebloans

Hundreds of years ago, the **Ancestral** Puebloan people lived in the cliffs that overlook Montezuma Valley in southwest Colorado. Families cooked, slept, and raised children in homes that they built into the rocks. Some were simple one-room **dwellings**. Others had more than fifty rooms. The clusters of homes now look like large, crumbling sandcastles.

Did you know?
The Ancestral Puebloans built their homes with sandstone bricks. They decorated the walls with colorful paints made from plants and minerals.

Mesa Verde National Park preserves these communities, or *pueblos*. The park is one of the most important **archeological** sites in the country. Researchers have found tools and other clues that tell stories of the Ancestral Puebloans. Visitors can explore the pueblos and learn all about the people who carved their lives into Colorado's land and history.

Fast Facts About Colorado

Colorado's Flag

The Colorado flag is deep blue with a white horizontal stripe across the center. These colors stand for the blue skies and white snow in Colorado. To the left of the center is a yellow circle that represents the state's sunshine. A large red C surrounds the circle.

State Flower
white and lavender
columbine

State Nickname:	The Centennial State
State Motto:	*Nil Sine Numine*; "Nothing Without Providence"
Year of Statehood:	1876
Capital City:	Denver
Other Major Cities:	Colorado Springs, Aurora, Fort Collins
Population:	5,029,196 (2010)
Area:	104,095 square miles (269,605 square kilometers); Colorado is the 8th largest state.
Major Industries:	manufacturing, services, farming
Natural Resources:	copper, coal, petroleum, natural gas, water
State Government:	65 representatives; 35 senators
Federal Government:	7 representatives; 2 senators
Electoral Votes:	9

State Animal
Rocky Mountain bighorn sheep

State Bird
lark bunting

Glossary

amphitheater—a circular theater with stadium seating around a stage

ancestral—relating to ancestors, or relatives who lived long ago

archeological—relating to the study of historic people and cultures

bareback—without a saddle

dwellings—homes or shelters

foothills—hills at the base of a mountain

ghost towns—towns or villages that have been abandoned

Great Plains—a region of flat or gently rolling land in the central United States; the Great Plains stretch over about one-third of the country.

hot springs—natural pools of hot water

Louisiana Purchase—a deal made between France and the United States; it gave the United States 828,000 square miles (2,144,510 square kilometers) of land west of the Mississippi River.

memorials—structures built to remember people or events

native—originally from a specific place

plains—larges areas of flat land

plateaus—areas of flat, raised land

rodeo—an event where people compete at tasks such as bull riding and calf roping; cowboys once completed these tasks as part of their daily work.

service jobs—jobs that perform tasks for people or businesses

summit—the highest point of a mountain

tourists—people who travel to visit another place

To Learn More

AT THE LIBRARY

Collins, Terry. *The Mesa Verde Cliff Dwellers: An Isabel Soto Archaeology Adventure*. Mankato, Minn.: Capstone Press, 2010.

Henty, G. A. *In the Heart of the Rockies: An Adventure on the Colorado River*. Mineola, N.Y.: Dover Publications, 2005.

McLuskey, Krista. *Colorado: The Centennial State*. New York, N.Y.: Weigl, 2012.

ON THE WEB

Learning more about Colorado is as easy as 1, 2, 3.

1. Go to www.factsurfer.com.

2. Enter "Colorado" into the search box.

3. Click the "Surf" button and you will see a list of related Web sites.

With factsurfer.com, finding more information is just a click away.

Index

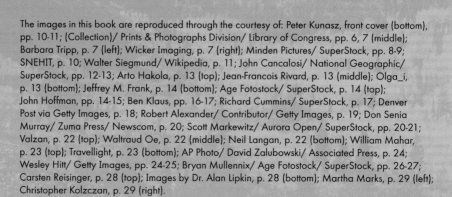